SciPy and NumPy

Eli Bressert

O'REILLY®

Beijing · Cambridge · Farnham · Köln · Sebastopol · Tokyo

SciPy and NumPy
by Eli Bressert

Published by O'Reilly Media, Inc., 1005 Gravenstein Highway North, Sebastopol, CA 95472.

O'Reilly books may be purchased for educational, business, or sales promotional use. Online editions are also available for most titles (*http://my.safaribooksonline.com*). For more information, contact our corporate/institutional sales department: (800) 998-9938 or *corporate@oreilly.com*.

Interior Designer:	David Futato		**Project Manager:**	Paul C. Anagnostopoulos
Cover Designer:	Randy Comer		**Copyeditor:**	MaryEllen N. Oliver
Editors:	Rachel Roumeliotis,		**Proofreader:**	Richard Camp
	Meghan Blanchette		**Illustrators:**	Eli Bressert, Laurel Muller
Production Editor:	Holly Bauer			

November 2012: First edition

Revision History for the First Edition:

2012-10-31   First release

See *http://oreilly.com/catalog/errata.csp?isbn=0636920020219* for release details.

ISBN: 978-1-449-30546-8
[LSI]

Table of Contents

Preface . . . . **v**

1. Introduction **1**

    1.1   Why SciPy and NumPy?   1

    1.2   Getting NumPy and SciPy   2

    1.3   Working with SciPy and NumPy   3

2. NumPy **5**

    2.1   NumPy Arrays   5

    2.2   Boolean Statements and NumPy Arrays   10

    2.3   Read and Write   12

    2.4   Math   14

3. SciPy **17**

    3.1   Optimization and Minimization   17

    3.2   Interpolation   22

    3.3   Integration   26

    3.4   Statistics   28

    3.5   Spatial and Clustering Analysis   32

    3.6   Signal and Image Processing   38

    3.7   Sparse Matrices   40

    3.8   Reading and Writing Files Beyond NumPy   41

4. SciKit: Taking SciPy One Step Further **43**

    4.1   Scikit-Image   43

    4.2   Scikit-Learn   48

5. Conclusion **55**

    5.1   Summary   55

    5.2   What's Next?   55

Preface

Python, a high-level language with easy-to-read syntax, is highly flexible, which makes it an ideal language to learn and use. For science and R&D, a few extra packages are used to streamline the development process and obtain goals with the fewest steps possible. Among the best of these are SciPy and NumPy. This book gives a brief overview of different tools in these two scientific packages, in order to jump start their use in the reader's own research projects.

NumPy and SciPy are the bread-and-butter Python extensions for numerical arrays and advanced data analysis. Hence, knowing what tools they contain and how to use them will make any programmer's life more enjoyable. This book will cover their uses, ranging from simple array creation to machine learning.

Audience

Anyone with basic (and upward) knowledge of Python is the targeted audience for this book. Although the tools in SciPy and NumPy are relatively advanced, using them is simple and should keep even a novice Python programmer happy.

Contents of this Book

This book covers the basics of SciPy and NumPy with some additional material. The first chapter describes what the SciPy and NumPy packages are, and how to access and install them on your computer. Chapter 2 goes over the basics of NumPy, starting with array creation. Chapter 3, which comprises the bulk of the book, covers a small sample of the voluminous SciPy toolbox. This chapter includes discussion and examples on integration, optimization, interpolation, and more. Chapter 4 discusses two well-known scikit packages: scikit-image and scikit-learn. These provide much more advanced material that can be immediately applied to real-world problems. In Chapter 5, the conclusion, we discuss what to do next for even more advanced material.

Conventions Used in This Book

The following typographical conventions are used in this book:

Plain text
> Indicates menu titles, menu options, menu buttons, and keyboard accelerators (such as Alt and Ctrl).

Italic
> Indicates new terms, URLs, email addresses, filenames, file extensions, pathnames, directories, and Unix utilities.

Constant width
> Indicates commands, options, switches, variables, attributes, keys, functions, types, classes, namespaces, methods, modules, properties, parameters, values, objects, events, event handlers, XML tags, HTML tags, macros, the contents of files, or the output from commands.

 This icon signifies a tip, suggestion, or general note.

 This icon indicates a warning or caution.

Using Code Examples

This book is here to help you get your job done. In general, you may use the code in this book in your programs and documentation. You do not need to contact us for permission unless you're reproducing a significant portion of the code. For example, writing a program that uses several chunks of code from this book does not require permission. Selling or distributing a CD-ROM of examples from O'Reilly books does require permission. Answering a question by citing this book and quoting example code does not require permission. Incorporating a significant amount of example code from this book into your product's documentation does require permission.

We appreciate, but do not require, attribution. An attribution usually includes the title, author, publisher, and ISBN. For example: "*SciPy and NumPy* by Eli Bressert (O'Reilly). Copyright 2013 Eli Bressert, 978-1-449-30546-8."

If you feel your use of code examples falls outside fair use or the permission given above, feel free to contact us at *permissions@oreilly.com*.

We'd Like to Hear from You

Please address comments and questions concerning this book to the publisher:

O'Reilly Media, Inc.
1005 Gravenstein Highway North
Sebastopol, CA 95472
(800) 998-9938 (in the United States or Canada)
(707) 829-0515 (international or local)
(707) 829-0104 (fax)

We have a web page for this book, where we list errata, examples, links to the code and data sets used, and any additional information. You can access this page at:

http://oreil.ly/SciPy_NumPy

To comment or ask technical questions about this book, send email to:

bookquestions@oreilly.com

For more information about our books, courses, conferences, and news, see our website at *http://www.oreilly.com*.

Find us on Facebook: *http://facebook.com/oreilly*

Follow us on Twitter: *http://twitter.com/oreillymedia*

Watch us on YouTube: *http://www.youtube.com/oreillymedia*

Safari® Books Online

Safari Books Online (*www.safaribooksonline.com*) is an on-demand digital library that delivers expert content in both book and video form from the world's leading authors in technology and business.

Technology professionals, software developers, web designers, and business and creative professionals use Safari Books Online as their primary resource for research, problem solving, learning, and certification training.

Safari Books Online offers a range of product mixes and pricing programs for organizations, government agencies, and individuals. Subscribers have access to thousands of books, training videos, and prepublication manuscripts in one fully searchable database from publishers like O'Reilly Media, Prentice Hall Professional, Addison-Wesley Professional, Microsoft Press, Sams, Que, Peachpit Press, Focal Press, Cisco Press, John Wiley & Sons, Syngress, Morgan Kaufmann, IBM Redbooks, Packt, Adobe Press, FT Press, Apress, Manning, New Riders, McGraw-Hill, Jones & Bartlett, Course Technology, and dozens more. For more information about Safari Books Online, please visit us online.

Acknowledgments

I would like to thank Meghan Blanchette and Julie Steele, my current and previous editors, for their patience, help, and expertise. This book wouldn't have materialized without their assistance. The tips, warnings, and package tools discussed in the book were much improved thanks to the two book reviewers: Tom Aldcroft and Sarah Kendrew. Colleagues and friends that have helped discuss certain aspects of this book and bolstered my drive to get it done are Leonardo Testi, Nate Bastian, Diederik Kruijssen, Joao Alves, Thomas Robitaille, and Farida Khatchadourian. A big thanks goes to my wife and son, Judith van Raalten and Taj Bressert, for their help and inspiration, and willingness to deal with me being huddled away behind the computer for endless hours.

## CHAPTER 1

Introduction

Python is a powerful programming language when considering portability, flexibility, syntax, style, and extendability. The language was written by Guido van Rossum with clean syntax built in. To define a function or initiate a loop, indentation is used instead of brackets. The result is profound: a Python programmer can look at any given uncommented Python code and quickly understand its inner workings and purpose.

Compiled languages like Fortran and C are natively much faster than Python, but not necessarily so when Python is bound to them. Using packages like *Cython* enables Python to interface with C code and pass information from the C program to Python and vice versa through memory. This allows Python to be on par with the faster languages when necessary and to use legacy code (e.g., *FFTW*). The combination of Python with fast computation has attracted scientists and others in large numbers. Two packages in particular are the powerhouses of scientific Python: NumPy and SciPy. Additionally, these two packages makes integrating legacy code easy.

1.1 Why SciPy and NumPy?

The basic operations used in scientific programming include arrays, matrices, integration, differential equation solvers, statistics, and much more. Python, by default, does not have any of these functionalities built in, except for some basic mathematical operations that can only deal with a variable and not an array or matrix. NumPy and SciPy are two powerful Python packages, however, that enable the language to be used efficiently for scientific purposes.

NumPy specializes in numerical processing through multi-dimensional `ndarrays`, where the arrays allow element-by-element operations, a.k.a. broadcasting. If needed, linear algebra formalism can be used without modifying the NumPy arrays beforehand. Moreover, the arrays can be modified in size dynamically. This takes out the worries that usually mire quick programming in other languages. Rather than creating a new array when you want to get rid of certain elements, you can apply a mask to it.

SciPy is built on the NumPy array framework and takes scientific programming to a whole new level by supplying advanced mathematical functions like integration, ordinary differential equation solvers, special functions, optimizations, and more. To list all the functions by name in SciPy would take several pages at minimum. When looking at the plethora of SciPy tools, it can sometimes be daunting even to decide which functions are best to use. That is why this book has been written. We will run through the primary and most often used tools, which will enable the reader to get results quickly and to explore the NumPy and SciPy packages with enough working knowledge to decide what is needed for problems that go beyond this book.

1.2   Getting NumPy and SciPy

Now you're probably sold and asking, "Great, where can I get and install these packages?" There are multiple ways to do this, and we will first go over the easiest ways for OS X, Linux, and Windows.

There are two well-known, comprehensive, precompiled Python packages that include NumPy and SciPy, and that work on all three platforms: the Enthought Python Distribution (EPD) and ActivePython (AP). If you would like the free versions of the two packages, you should download EPD Free[1] or AP Community Edition.[2] If you need support, then you can always opt for the more comprehensive packages from the two sources.

Optionally, if you are a MacPorts[3] user, you can install NumPy and SciPy through the package manager. Use the MacPorts command as given below to install the Python packages. Note that installing SciPy and NumPy with MacPorts will take time, especially with the SciPy package, so it's a good idea to initiate the installation procedure and go grab a cup of tea.

```
sudo port install py27-numpy py27-scipy py27-ipython
```

MacPorts supports several versions of Python (e.g., 2.6 and 2.7). So, although py27 is listed above, if you would like to use Python 2.6 instead with SciPy and NumPy then you would simply replace py27 with py26.

If you're using a Debian-based Linux distro like Ubuntu or Linux Mint, then use apt-get to install the packages.

```
sudo apt-get install python-numpy python-scipy
```

With an RPM-based system like Fedora or OpenSUSE, you can install the Python packages using yum.

```
sudo yum install numpy scipy
```

---

[1] *http://www.enthought.com/products/epd_free.php*

[2] *http://www.activestate.com/activepython/downloads*

[3] *www.macports.com*

Building and installing NumPy and SciPy on Windows systems is more complicated than on the Unix-based systems, as code compilation is tricky. Fortunately, there is an excellent compiled binary installation program called python(x,y)[4] that has both NumPy and SciPy included and is Windows specific.

For those who prefer building NumPy and SciPy from source, visit *www.scipy.org/ Download* to download from either the stable or bleeding-edge repositories. Or clone the code repositories from *scipy.github.com* and *numpy.github.com*. Unless you're a pro at building packages from source code and relish the challenge, though, I would recommend sticking with the precompiled package options as listed above.

1.3   Working with SciPy and NumPy

You can work with Python programs in two different ways: interactively or through scripts. Some programmers swear that it is best to script all your code, so you don't have to redo tedious tasks again when needed. Others say that interactive programming is the way to go, as you can explore the functionalities inside out. I would vouch for both, personally. If you have a terminal with the Python environment open and a text editor to write your script, you get the best of both worlds.

For the interactive component, I *highly* recommend using IPython.[5] It takes the best of the bash environment (e.g., using the tab button to complete a command and changing directories) and combines it with the Python environment. It does far more than this, but for the purpose of the examples in this book it should be enough to get it up and running.

Bugs in programs are a fact of life and there's no way around them. Being able to find bugs and fix them quickly and easily is a big part of successful programming. IPython contains a feature where you can debug a buggy Python script by typing **debug** after running it. See *http:/ /ipython.org/ipython-doc/stable/interactive/tutorial.html* for details under the debugging section.

---

[4] *http://code.google.com/p/pythonxy/*

[5] *http://ipython.org/*

## CHAPTER 2

NumPy

2.1 NumPy Arrays

NumPy is the fundamental Python package for scientific computing. It adds the capabilities of N-dimensional arrays, element-by-element operations (broadcasting), core mathematical operations like linear algebra, and the ability to wrap C/C++/Fortran code. We will cover most of these aspects in this chapter by first covering what NumPy arrays are, and their advantages versus Python lists and dictionaries.

Python stores data in several different ways, but the most popular methods are *lists* and *dictionaries*. The Python `list` object can store nearly any type of Python object as an element. But operating on the elements in a list can only be done through iterative loops, which is computationally inefficient in Python. The NumPy package enables users to overcome the shortcomings of the Python lists by providing a data storage object called `ndarray`.

The `ndarray` is similar to lists, but rather than being highly flexible by storing different types of objects in one list, only the same type of element can be stored in each column. For example, with a Python list, you could make the first element a list and the second another list or dictionary. With NumPy arrays, you can only store the same type of element, e.g., all elements must be floats, integers, or strings. Despite this limitation, `ndarray` wins hands down when it comes to operation times, as the operations are sped up significantly. Using the `%timeit` magic command in IPython, we compare the power of NumPy `ndarray` versus Python lists in terms of speed.

```
import numpy as np

# Create an array with 10^7 elements.
arr = np.arange(1e7)

# Converting ndarray to list
larr = arr.tolist()

# Lists cannot by default broadcast,
# so a function is coded to emulate
# what an ndarray can do.
```

```
def list_times(alist, scalar):
    for i, val in enumerate(alist):
        alist[i] = val * scalar
    return alist

# Using IPython's magic timeit command
timeit arr * 1.1
>>> 1 loops, best of 3: 76.9 ms per loop

timeit list_times(larr, 1.1)
>>> 1 loops, best of 3: 2.03 s per loop
```

The ndarray operation is ~ 25 faster than the Python loop in this example. Are you convinced that the NumPy ndarray is the way to go? From this point on, we will be working with the array objects instead of lists when possible.

Should we need linear algebra operations, we can use the matrix object, which does not use the default broadcast operation from ndarray. For example, when you multiply two equally sized ndarrays, which we will denote as A and B, the $n_{i,j}$ element of A is only multiplied by the $n_{i,j}$ element of B. When multiplying two matrix objects, the usual matrix multiplication operation is executed.

Unlike the ndarray objects, matrix objects can and only will be two dimensional. This means that trying to construct a third or higher dimension is not possible. Here's an example.

```
import numpy as np

# Creating a 3D numpy array
arr = np.zeros((3,3,3))

# Trying to convert array to a matrix, which will not work
mat = np.matrix(arr)

# "ValueError: shape too large to be a matrix."
```

If you are working with matrices, keep this in mind.

2.1.1 Array Creation and Data Typing

There are many ways to create an array in NumPy, and here we will discuss the ones that are most useful.

```
# First we create a list and then
# wrap it with the np.array() function.
alist = [1, 2, 3]
arr = np.array(alist)

# Creating an array of zeros with five elements
arr = np.zeros(5)

# What if we want to create an array going from 0 to 100?
arr = np.arange(100)
```

```
# Or 10 to 100?
arr = np.arange(10,100)

# If you want 100 steps from 0 to 1...
arr = np.linspace(0, 1, 100)

# Or if you want to generate an array from 1 to 10
# in log10 space in 100 steps...
arr = np.logspace(0, 1, 100, base=10.0)

# Creating a 5x5 array of zeros (an image)
image = np.zeros((5,5))

# Creating a 5x5x5 cube of 1's
# The astype() method sets the array with integer elements.
cube = np.zeros((5,5,5)).astype(int) + 1

# Or even simpler with 16-bit floating-point precision...
cube = np.ones((5, 5, 5)).astype(np.float16)
```

When generating arrays, NumPy will default to the bit depth of the Python environment. If you are working with 64-bit Python, then your elements in the arrays will default to 64-bit precision. This precision takes a fair chunk memory and is not always necessary. You can specify the bit depth when creating arrays by setting the data type parameter (dtype) to int, numpy.float16, numpy.float32, or numpy.float64. Here's an example how to do it.

```
# Array of zero integers
arr = np.zeros(2, dtype=int)

# Array of zero floats
arr = np.zeros(2, dtype=np.float32)
```

Now that we have created arrays, we can reshape them in many other ways. If we have a 25-element array, we can make it a 5 × 5 array, or we could make a 3-dimensional array from a flat array.

```
# Creating an array with elements from 0 to 999
arr1d = np.arange(1000)

# Now reshaping the array to a 10x10x10 3D array
arr3d = arr1d.reshape((10,10,10))

# The reshape command can alternatively be called this way
arr3d = np.reshape(arr1s, (10, 10, 10))

# Inversely, we can flatten arrays
arr4d = np.zeros((10, 10, 10, 10))
arr1d = arr4d.ravel()

print arr1d.shape
        (1000,)
```

The possibilities for restructuring the arrays are large and, most importantly, easy.

Keep in mind that the restructured arrays above are just different views of the same data in memory. This means that if you modify one of the arrays, it will modify the others. For example, if you set the first element of `arr1d` from the example above to 1, then the first element of `arr3d` will also become 1. If you don't want this to happen, then use the `numpy.copy` function to separate the arrays memory-wise.

2.1.2   Record Arrays

Arrays are generally collections of integers or floats, but sometimes it is useful to store more complex data structures where columns are composed of different data types. In research journal publications, tables are commonly structured so that some columns may have string characters for identification and floats for numerical quantities. Being able to store this type of information is very beneficial. In NumPy there is the `numpy.recarray`. Constructing a `recarray` for the first time can be a bit confusing, so we will go over the basics below. The first example comes from the NumPy documentation on record arrays.

```
# Creating an array of zeros and defining column types
recarr = np.zeros((2,), dtype=('i4,f4,a10'))
toadd = [(1,2.,'Hello'),(2,3.,"World")]
recarr[:] = toadd
```

The `dtype` optional argument is defining the types designated for the first to third columns, where `i4` corresponds to a 32-bit integer, `f4` corresponds to a 32-bit float, and `a10` corresponds to a string 10 characters long. Details on how to define more types can be found in the NumPy documentation.[1] This example illustrates what the `recarray` looks like, but it is hard to see how we could populate such an array easily. Thankfully, in Python there is a global function called `zip` that will create a list of tuples like we see above for the `toadd` object. So we show how to use `zip` to populate the same `recarray`.

```
# Creating an array of zeros and defining column types
recarr = np.zeros((2,), dtype=('i4,f4,a10'))

# Now creating the columns we want to put
# in the recarray
col1 = np.arange(2) + 1
col2 = np.arange(2, dtype=np.float32)
col3 = ['Hello', 'World']

# Here we create a list of tuples that is
# identical to the previous toadd list.
toadd = zip(col1, col2, col3)

# Assigning values to recarr
recarr[:] = toadd
```

[1] *http://docs.scipy.org/doc/numpy/user/basics.rec.html*

```
# Assigning names to each column, which
# are now by default called 'f0', 'f1', and 'f2'.

recarr.dtype.names = ('Integers' , 'Floats', 'Strings')

# If we want to access one of the columns by its name, we
# can do the following.

recarr('Integers')
# array([1, 2], dtype=int32)
```

The **recarray** structure may appear a bit tedious to work with, but this will become more important later on, when we cover how to read in complex data with NumPy in the *Read and Write* section.

 If you are doing research in astronomy or astrophysics and you commonly work with data tables, there is a high-level package called ATpy[2] that would be of interest. It allows the user to read, write, and convert data tables from/to FITS, ASCII, HDF5, and SQL formats.

2.1.3 Indexing and Slicing

Python index lists begin at zero and the NumPy arrays follow suit. When indexing lists in Python, we normally do the following for a 2 × 2 object:

```
alist=[[1,2],[3,4]]

# To return the (0,1) element we must index as shown below.
alist[0][1]
```

If we want to return the right-hand column, there is no trivial way to do so with Python lists. In NumPy, indexing follows a more convenient syntax.

```
# Converting the list defined above into an array
arr = np.array(alist)

# To return the (0,1) element we use ...
arr[0,1]

# Now to access the last column, we simply use ...
arr[:,1]

# Accessing the columns is achieved in the same way,
# which is the bottom row.
arr[1,:]
```

Sometimes there are more complex indexing schemes required, such as conditional indexing. The most commonly used type is numpy.where(). With this function you can return the desired indices from an array, regardless of its dimensions, based on some conditions(s).

---

[2] *http://atpy.github.com*

```
# Creating an array
arr = np.arange(5)

# Creating the index array
index = np.where(arr > 2)
print(index)
    (array([3, 4]),)

# Creating the desired array
new_arr = arr[index]
```

However, you may want to remove specific indices instead. To do this you can use numpy.delete(). The required input variables are the array and indices that you want to remove.

```
# We use the previous array
new_arr = np.delete(arr, index)
```

Instead of using the numpy.where function, we can use a simple boolean array to return specific elements.

```
index = arr > 2
print(index)
    [False False True True True]
new_arr = arr[index]
```

Which method is better and when should we use one over the other? If speed is important, the boolean indexing is faster for a large number of elements. Additionally, you can easily invert True and False objects in an array by using ~ index, a technique that is far faster than redoing the numpy.where function.

2.2   Boolean Statements and NumPy Arrays

Boolean statements are commonly used in combination with the and operator and the or operator. These operators are useful when comparing single boolean values to one another, but when using NumPy arrays, you can only use & and | as this allows fast comparisons of boolean values. Anyone familiar with formal logic will see that what we can do with NumPy is a natural extension to working with arrays. Below is an example of indexing using compound boolean statements, which are visualized in three subplots (see Figure 2-1) for context.

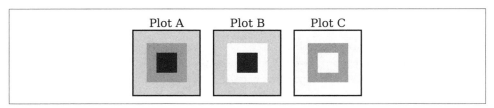

Figure 2-1. Three plots showing how indexing with NumPy works.

```
# Creating an image
img1 = np.zeros((20, 20)) + 3
img1[4:-4, 4:-4] = 6
img1[7:-7, 7:-7] = 9
# See Plot A

# Let's filter out all values larger than 2 and less than 6.
index1 = img1 > 2
index2 = img1 < 6
compound_index = index1 & index2

# The compound statement can alternatively be written as
compound_index = (img1 > 3) & (img1 < 7)
img2 = np.copy(img1)
img2[compound_index] = 0
# See Plot B.

# Making the boolean arrays even more complex
index3 = img1 == 9
index4 = (index1 & index2) | index3
img3 = np.copy(img1)
img3[index4] = 0
# See Plot C.
```

 When constructing complex boolean arguments, it is important to use parentheses. Just as with the order of operations in math (PEMDAS), you need to organize the boolean arguments contained to construct the right logical statements.

Alternatively, in a special case where you only want to operate on specific elements in an array, doing so is quite simple.

```
import numpy as np
import numpy.random as rand

# Creating a 100-element array with random values
# from a standard normal distribution or, in other
# words, a Gaussian distribution.
# The sigma is 1 and the mean is 0.
a = rand.randn(100)

# Here we generate an index for filtering
# out undesired elements.
index = a > 0.2
b = a[index]

# We execute some operation on the desired elements.
b = b ** 2 - 2

# Then we put the modified elements back into the
# original array.
a[index] = b
```

2.3   Read and Write

Reading and writing information from data files, be it in text or binary format, is crucial for scientific computing. It provides the ability to save, share, and read data that is computed by any language. Fortunately, Python is quite capable of reading and writing data.

2.3.1   Text Files

In terms of text files, Python is one of the most capable programming languages. Not only is the parsing robust and flexible, but it is also fast compared to other languages like C. Here's an example of how Python opens and parses text information.

```
# Opening the text file with the 'r' option,
# which only allows reading capability
f = open('somefile.txt', 'r')

# Parsing the file and splitting each line,
# which creates a list where each element of
# it is one line
alist = f.readlines()

# Closing file
f.close()
.
.
.
# After a few operations, we open a new text file
# to write the data with the 'w' option. If there
# was data already existing in the file, it will be overwritten.
f = open('newtextfile.txt', 'w')

# Writing data to file
f.writelines(newdata)

# Closing file
f.close()
```

Accessing and recording data this way can be very flexible and fast, but there is one downside: if the file is large, then accessing or modulating the data will be cumbersome and slow. Getting the data directly into a `numpy.ndarray` would be the best option. We can do this by using a NumPy function called `loadtxt`. If the data is structured with rows and columns, then the `loadtxt` command will work very well as long as all the data is of a similar type, i.e., integers or floats. We can save the data through `numpy.savetxt` as easily and quickly as with `numpy.readtxt`.

```
import numpy as np

arr = np.loadtxt('somefile.txt')

np.savetxt('somenewfile.txt')
```

If each column is different in terms of formatting, `loadtxt` can still read the data, but the column types need to be predefined. The final construct from reading the data will be a **recarray**. Here we run through a simple example to get an idea of how NumPy deals with this more complex data structure.

```
# example.txt file looks like the following
#
# XR21 32.789 1
# XR22 33.091 2

table = np.loadtxt('example.txt',
            dtype='names': ('ID', 'Result', 'Type'),
            'formats': ('S4', 'f4', 'i2'))

# array([('XR21', 32.78900146484375, 1),
#        ('XR22', 33.090999603271484, 2)],
# dtype=[('ID', '|S4'), ('Result', '<f4'), ('Type', '<i2')])
```

Just as in the earlier material covering **recarray** objects, we can access each column by its name, e.g., `table['Result']`. Accessing each row is done the same was as with normal `numpy.array` objects.

There is one downside to **recarray** objects, though: as of version NumPy 1.8, there is no dependable and automated way to save `numpy.recarray` data structures in text format. If saving **recarray** structures is important, it is best to use the `matplotlib.mlab`[3] tools.

 There is a highly generalized and fast text parsing/writing package called Asciitable.[4] If reading and writing data in ASCII format is frequently needed for your work, this is a must-have package to use with NumPy.

2.3.2   Binary Files

Text files are an excellent way to read, transfer, and store data due to their built-in portability and user friendliness for viewing. Binary files in retrospect are harder to deal with, as formatting, readability, and portability are trickier. Yet they have two notable advantages over text-based files: file size and read/write speeds. This is especially important when working with big data.

In NumPy, files can be accessed in binary format using `numpy.save` and `numpy.load`. The primary limitation is that the binary format is only readable to other systems that are using NumPy. If you want to read and write files in a more portable format, then `scipy.io` will do the job. This will be covered in the next chapter. For the time being, let us review NumPy's capabilities.

```
import numpy as np

# Creating a large array
data = np.empty((1000, 1000))
```

---

[3] *http://matplotlib.sourceforge.net/api/mlab_api.html*
[4] *http://cxc.harvard.edu/contrib/asciitable/*

```
# Saving the array with numpy.save
np.save('test.npy', data)

# If space is an issue for large files, then
# use numpy.savez instead. It is slower than
# numpy.save because it compresses the binary
# file.
np.savez('test.npz', data)

# Loading the data array
newdata = np.load('test.npy')
```

Fortunately, `numpy.save` and `numpy.savez` have no issues saving `numpy.recarray` objects. Hence, working with complex and structured arrays is no issue if portability beyond the Python environment is not of concern.

2.4   Math

Python comes with its own `math` module that works on Python native objects. Unfortunately, if you try to use `math.cos` on a NumPy array, it will not work, as the `math` functions are meant to operate on elements and not on lists or arrays. Hence, NumPy comes with its own set of math tools. These are optimized to work with NumPy array objects and operate at fast speeds. When importing NumPy, most of the math tools are automatically included, from simple trigonometric and logarithmic functions to the more complex, such as fast Fourier transform (FFT) and linear algebraic operations.

2.4.1   Linear Algebra

NumPy arrays do not behave like matrices in linear algebra by default. Instead, the operations are mapped from each element in one array onto the next. This is quite a useful feature, as loop operations can be done away with for efficiency. But what about when transposing or a dot multiplication are needed? Without invoking other classes, you can use the built-in `numpy.dot` and `numpy.transpose` to do such operations. The syntax is Pythonic, so it is intuitive to program. Or the math purist can use the `numpy.matrix` object instead. We will go over both examples below to illustrate the differences and similarities between the two options. More importantly, we will compare some of the advantages and disadvantages between the `numpy.array` and the `numpy.matrix` objects.

Some operations are easy and quick to do in linear algebra. A classic example is solving a system of equations that we can express in matrix form:

$$3x + 6y - 5z = 12$$
$$x - 3y + 2z = -2 \tag{2.1}$$
$$5x - y + 4z = 10$$

$$\begin{bmatrix} 3 & 6 & -5 \\ 1 & -3 & 2 \\ 5 & -1 & 4 \end{bmatrix} \begin{bmatrix} x \\ y \\ z \end{bmatrix} = \begin{bmatrix} 12 \\ -2 \\ 10 \end{bmatrix} \tag{2.2}$$

Now let us represent the matrix system as $\mathbf{AX} = \mathbf{B}$, and solve for the variables. This means we should try to obtain $\mathbf{X} = \mathbf{A}^{-1}\mathbf{B}$. Here is how we would do this with NumPy.

```python
import numpy as np

# Defining the matrices
A = np.matrix([[3, 6, -5],
               [1, -3, 2],
               [5, -1, 4]])

B = np.matrix([[12],
               [-2],
               [10]])

# Solving for the variables, where we invert A
X = A ** (-1) * B
print(X)

# matrix([[ 1.75],
#    [ 1.75],
#    [ 0.75]])
```

The solutions for the variables are $x = 1.75$, $y = 1.75$, and $z = 0.75$. You can easily check this by executing $\mathbf{AX}$, which should produce the same elements defined in $\mathbf{B}$. Doing this sort of operation with NumPy is easy, as such a system can be expanded to much larger 2D matrices.

Not all matrices are invertible, so this method of solving for solutions in a system does not always work. You can sidestep this problem by using `numpy.linalg.svd`,[5] which usually works well inverting poorly conditioned matrices.

Now that we understand how NumPy matrices work, we can show how to do the same operations without specifically using the `numpy.matrix` subclass. (The `numpy.matrix` subclass is contained within the `numpy.array` class, which means that we can do the same example as that above without directly invoking the `numpy.matrix` class.)

```python
import numpy as np

a = np.array([[3, 6, -5],
              [1, -3, 2],
              [5, -1, 4]])

# Defining the array
b = np.array([12, -2, 10])

# Solving for the variables, where we invert A
x = np.linalg.inv(a).dot(b)
print(x)

# array([ 1.75,  1.75,  0.75])
```

---

[5] *http://docs.scipy.org/doc/numpy/reference/generated/numpy.linalg.svd.html*

Both methods of approaching linear algebra operations are viable, but which one is the best? The `numpy.matrix` method is syntactically the simplest. However, `numpy.array` is the most practical. First, the NumPy array is the standard for using nearly anything in the scientific Python environment, so bugs pertaining to the linear algebra operations will be less frequent than with `numpy.matrix` operations. Furthermore, in examples such as the two shown above, the `numpy.array` method is computationally faster.

Passing data structures from one class to another can become cumbersome and lead to unexpected results when not done correctly. This would likely happen if one were to use `numpy.matrix` and then pass it to `numpy.array` for further operations. Sticking with one data structure will lead to fewer headaches and less worry than switching between matrices and arrays. It is advisable, then, to use `numpy.array` whenever possible.

## CHAPTER 3

SciPy

With NumPy we can achieve fast solutions with simple coding. Where does SciPy come into the picture? It's a package that utilizes NumPy arrays and manipulations to take on standard problems that scientists and engineers commonly face: integration, determining a function's maxima or minima, finding eigenvectors for large sparse matrices, testing whether two distributions are the same, and much more. We will cover just the basics here, which will allow you to take advantage of the more complex features in SciPy by going through easy examples that are applicable to real-world problems.

We will start with optimization and data fitting, as these are some of the most common tasks, and then move through interpolation, integration, spatial analysis, clustering, signal and image processing, sparse matrices, and statistics.

3.1 Optimization and Minimization

The optimization package in SciPy allows us to solve minimization problems easily and quickly. But wait: what is minimization and how can it help you with your work? Some classic examples are performing linear regression, finding a function's minimum and maximum values, determining the root of a function, and finding where two functions intersect. Below we begin with a simple linear regression and then expand it to fitting non-linear data.

 The optimization and minimization tools that NumPy and SciPy provide are great, but they do not have Markov Chain Monte Carlo (MCMC) capabilities—in other words, Bayesian analysis. There are several popular MCMC Python packages like PyMC,[1] a rich package with many options, and emcee,[2] an affine invariant MCMC ensemble sampler (meaning that large scales are not a problem for it).

---

[1] *http://pymc-devs.github.com/pymc/*

[2] *http://danfm.ca/emcee/*

3.1.1 Data Modeling and Fitting

There are several ways to fit data with a linear regression. In this section we will use curve_fit, which is a χ^2-based method (in other words, a best-fit method). In the example below, we generate data from a known function with noise, and then fit the noisy data with curve_fit. The function we will model in the example is a simple linear equation, $f(x) = ax + b$.

```python
import numpy as np
from scipy.optimize import curve_fit

# Creating a function to model and create data
def func(x, a, b):
    return a * x + b

# Generating clean data
x = np.linspace(0, 10, 100)
y = func(x, 1, 2)

# Adding noise to the data
yn = y + 0.9 * np.random.normal(size=len(x))

# Executing curve_fit on noisy data
popt, pcov = curve_fit(func, x, yn)

# popt returns the best fit values for parameters of
# the given model (func).

print(popt)
```

The values from popt, if a good fit, should be close to the values for the y assignment. You can check the quality of the fit with pcov, where the diagonal elements are the variances for each parameter. Figure 3-1 gives a visual illustration of the fit.

Taking this a step further, we can do a least-squares fit to a Gaussian profile, a non-linear function:

$$a * \exp\left(\frac{-(x - \mu)^2}{2\,\sigma^2}\right),$$

where a is a scalar, μ is the mean, and σ is the standard deviation.

```python
# Creating a function to model and create data
def func(x, a, b, c):
    return a*np.exp(-(x-b)**2/(2*c**2))

# Generating clean data
x = np.linspace(0, 10, 100)
y = func(x, 1, 5, 2)

# Adding noise to the data
yn = y + 0.2 * np.random.normal(size=len(x))

# Executing curve_fit on noisy data
popt, pcov = curve_fit(func, x, yn)
```

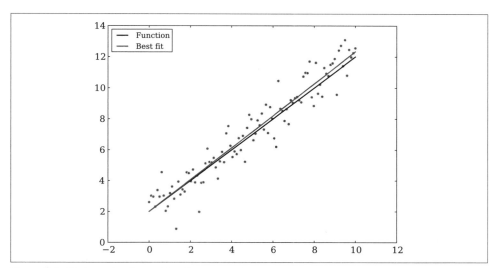

Figure 3-1. Fitting noisy data with a linear equation.

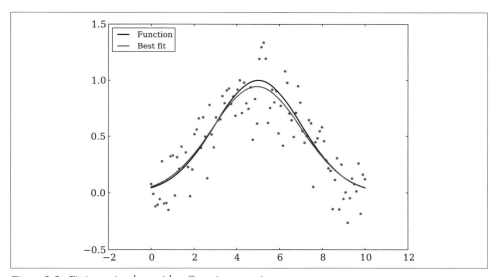

Figure 3-2. Fitting noisy data with a Gaussian equation.

```
# popt returns the best-fit values for parameters of the given model (func).
print(popt)
```

As we can see in Figure 3-2, the result from the Gaussian fit is acceptable.

Going one more step, we can fit a one-dimensional dataset with multiple Gaussian profiles. The func is now expanded to include two Gaussian equations with different input variables. This example would be the classic case of fitting line spectra (see Figure 3-3).

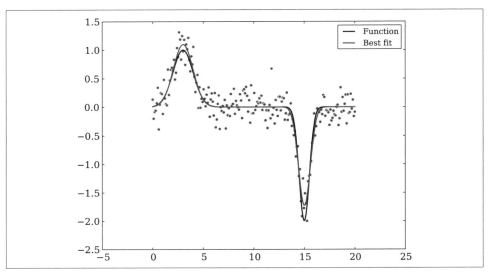

Figure 3-3. Fitting noisy data with multiple Gaussian equations.

```
# Two-Gaussian model
def func(x, a0, b0, c0, a1, b1,c1):
    return a0*np.exp(-(x - b0) ** 2/(2 * c0 ** 2))\
           + a1 * np.exp(-(x - b1) ** 2/(2 * c1 ** 2))

# Generating clean data
x = np.linspace(0, 20, 200)
y = func(x, 1, 3, 1, -2, 15, 0.5)

# Adding noise to the data
yn = y + 0.2 * np.random.normal(size=len(x))

# Since we are fitting a more complex function,
# providing guesses for the fitting will lead to
# better results.

guesses = [1, 3, 1, 1, 15, 1]
# Executing curve_fit on noisy data
popt, pcov = curve_fit(func, x, yn,
                       p0=guesses)
```

3.1.2   Solutions to Functions

With data modeling and fitting under our belts, we can move on to finding solutions, such as "What is the root of a function?" or "Where do two functions intersect?" SciPy provides an arsenal of tools to do this in the optimize module. We will run through the primary ones in this section.

Let's start simply, by solving for the root of an equation (see Figure 3-4). Here we will use scipy.optimize.fsolve.

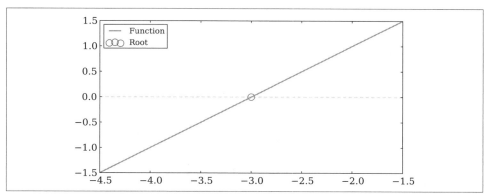

Figure 3-4. Approximate the root of a linear function at y = 0.

```
from scipy.optimize import fsolve
import numpy as np

line = lambda x: x + 3

solution = fsolve(line, -2)
print solution
```

Finding the intersection points between two equations is nearly as simple.[3]

```
from scipy.optimize import fsolve
import numpy as np

# Defining function to simplify intersection solution
def findIntersection(func1, func2, x0):
    return fsolve(lambda x : func1(x) - func2(x), x0)

# Defining functions that will intersect
funky = lambda x : np.cos(x / 5) * np.sin(x / 2)
line = lambda x : 0.01 * x - 0.5

# Defining range and getting solutions on intersection points
x = np.linspace(0,45,10000)
result = findIntersection(funky, line, [15, 20, 30, 35, 40, 45])

# Printing out results for x and y
print(result, line(result))
```

As we can see in Figure 3-5, the intersection points are well identified. Keep in mind that the assumptions about where the functions will intersect are important. If these are incorrect, you could get specious results.

---

[3] This is a modified example from *http://glowingpython.blogspot.de/2011/05/hot-to-find-intersection-of-two.html*.

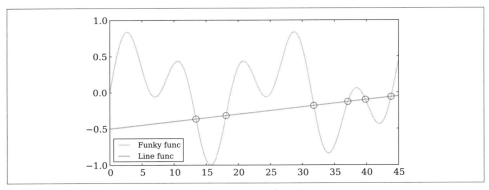

Figure 3-5. Finding the intersection points between two functions.

3.2 Interpolation

Data that contains information usually has a functional form, and as analysts we want to model it. Given a set of sample data, obtaining the intermediate values between the points is useful to understand and predict what the data will do in the non-sampled domain. SciPy offers well over a dozen different functions for interpolation, ranging from those for simple univariate cases to those for complex multivariate ones. Univariate interpolation is used when the sampled data is likely led by one independent variable, whereas multivariate interpolation assumes there is more than one independent variable.

There are two basic methods of interpolation: (1) Fit one function to an entire dataset or (2) fit different parts of the dataset with several functions where the joints of each function are joined smoothly. The second type is known as a spline interpolation, which can be a very powerful tool when the functional form of data is complex. We will first show how to interpolate a simple function, and then proceed to a more complex case. The example below interpolates a sinusoidal function (see Figure 3-6) using `scipy.interpolate.interp1d` with different fitting parameters. The first parameter is a "linear" fit and the second is a "quadratic" fit.

```
import numpy as np
from scipy.interpolate import interp1d

# Setting up fake data
x = np.linspace(0, 10 * np.pi, 20)
y = np.cos(x)

# Interpolating data
fl = interp1d(x, y, kind='linear')
fq = interp1d(x, y, kind='quadratic')

# x.min and x.max are used to make sure we do not
# go beyond the boundaries of the data for the
# interpolation.
xint = np.linspace(x.min(), x.max(), 1000)
yintl = fl(xint)
yintq = fq(xint)
```

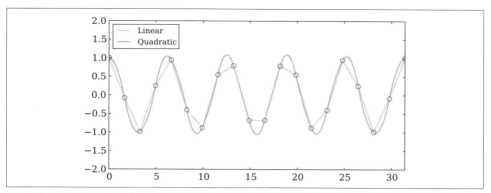

Figure 3-6. Synthetic data points (red dots) interpolated with linear and quadratic parameters.

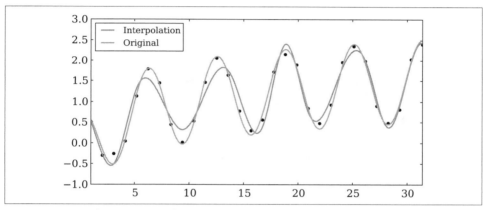

Figure 3-7. Interpolating noisy synthetic data.

 Figure 3-6 shows that in this case the quadratic fit is far better. This should demonstrate how important it is to choose the proper parameters when interpolating data.

Can we interpolate noisy data? Yes, and it is surprisingly easy, using a spline-fitting function called `scipy.interpolate.UnivariateSpline`. (The result is shown in Figure 3-7.)

```python
import numpy as np
import matplotlib.pyplot as mpl
from scipy.interpolate import UnivariateSpline

# Setting up fake data with artificial noise
sample = 30
x = np.linspace(1, 10 * np.pi, sample)
y = np.cos(x) + np.log10(x) + np.random.randn(sample) / 10

# Interpolating the data
f = UnivariateSpline(x, y, s=1)
```

```
# x.min and x.max are used to make sure we do not
# go beyond the boundaries of the data for the
# interpolation.
xint = np.linspace(x.min(), x.max(), 1000)
yint = f(xint)
```

The option s is the smoothing factor, which should be used when fitting data with noise. If instead s=0, then the interpolation will go through all points while ignoring noise.

Last but not least, we go over a multivariate example—in this case, to reproduce an image. The scipy.interpolate.griddata function is used for its capacity to deal with unstructured *N*-dimensional data. For example, if you have a 1000 × 1000-pixel image, and then randomly selected 1000 points, how well could you reconstruct the image? Refer to Figure 3-8 to see how well *scipy.interpolate.griddata performs*.

```
import numpy as np
from scipy.interpolate import griddata

# Defining a function
ripple = lambda x, y: np.sqrt(x**2 + y**2)+np.sin(x**2 + y**2)

# Generating gridded data. The complex number defines
# how many steps the grid data should have. Without the
# complex number mgrid would only create a grid data structure
# with 5 steps.
grid_x, grid_y = np.mgrid[0:5:1000j, 0:5:1000j]

# Generating sample that interpolation function will see
xy = np.random.rand(1000, 2)
sample = ripple(xy[:,0] * 5 , xy[:,1] * 5)

# Interpolating data with a cubic
grid_z0 = griddata(xy * 5, sample, (grid_x, grid_y), method='cubic')
```

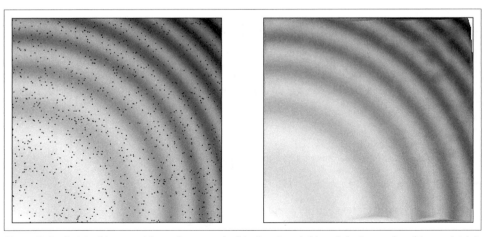

Figure 3-8. Original image with random sample (black points, left) and the interpolated image (right).

On the left-hand side of Figure 3-8 is the original image; the black points are the randomly sampled positions. On the right-hand side is the interpolated image. There are some slight glitches that come from the sample being too sparse for the finer structures. The only way to get a better interpolation is with a larger sample size. (Note that the `griddata` function has been recently added to SciPy and is only available for version 0.9 and beyond.)

If we employ another multivariate spline interpolation, how would its results compare? Here we use `scipy.interpolate.SmoothBivariateSpline`, where the code is quite similar to that in the previous example.

```
import numpy as np
from scipy.interpolate import SmoothBivariateSpline as SBS

# Defining a function
ripple = lambda x, y: np.sqrt(x**2 + y**2)+np.sin(x**2 + y**2)

# Generating sample that interpolation function will see
xy= np.random.rand(1000, 2)
x, y = xy[:,0], xy[:,1]
sample = ripple(xy[:,0] * 5 , xy[:,1] * 5)

# Interpolating data
fit = SBS(x * 5, y * 5, sample, s=0.01, kx=4, ky=4)
interp = fit(np.linspace(0, 5, 1000), np.linspace(0, 5, 1000))
```

We have a similar result to that in the last example (Figure 3-9). The left panel shows the original image with randomly sampled points, and in the right panel is the interpolated data. The `SmoothBivariateSpline` function appears to work a bit better than `griddata`, with an exception in the upper-right corner.

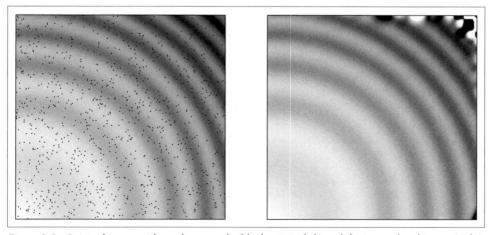

Figure 3-9. Original image with random sample (black points, left) and the interpolated image (right).

Although from the figure SmoothBivariateSpline does appear to work better, run the code several times to see what happens. SmoothBivariate-Spline is very sensitive to the data sample it is given, and interpolations can go way off the mark. griddata is more robust and can produce a reasonable interpolation regardless of the data sample it is given.

3.3 Integration

Integration is a crucial tool in math and science, as differentiation and integration are the two key components of calculus. Given a curve from a function or a dataset, we can calculate the area below it. In the traditional classroom setting we would integrate a function analytically, but data in the research setting is rarely given in this form, and we need to approximate its definite integral.

The main purpose of integration with SciPy is to obtain numerical solutions. If you need indefinite integral solutions, then you should look at SymPy.[4] It solves mathematical problems symbolically for many types of computation beyond calculus.

SciPy has a range of different functions to integrate equations and data. We will first go over these functions, and then move on to the data solutions. Afterward, we will employ the data-fitting tools we used earlier to compute definite integral solutions.

3.3.1 Analytic Integration

We will begin working with the function expressed below. It is straightforward to integrate and its solution's estimated error is small. See Figure 3-10 for the visual context of what is being calculated.

$$\int_0^3 \cos^2(e^x)\, dx \tag{3.1}$$

```
import numpy as np
from scipy.integrate import quad

# Defining function to integrate
func = lambda x: np.cos(np.exp(x)) ** 2

# Integrating function with upper and lower
# limits of 0 and 3, respectively
solution = quad(func, 0, 3)
print solution

# The first element is the desired value
# and the second is the error.
# (1.296467785724373, 1.397797186265988e-09)
```

---

[4] http://sympy.org/en/index.html

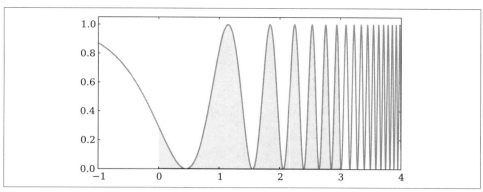

Figure 3-10. Definite integral (shaded region) of a function.

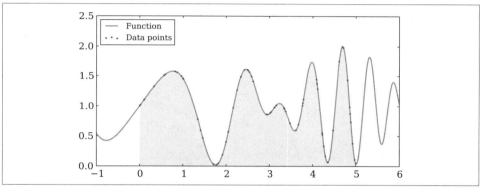

Figure 3-11. Definite integral (shaded region) of a function. The original function is the line and the randomly sampled data points are in red.

3.3.2   Numerical Integration

Let's move on to a problem where we are given data instead of some known equation and numerical integration is needed. Figure 3-11 illustrates what type of data sample can be used to approximate acceptable indefinite integrals.

```python
import numpy as np
from scipy.integrate import quad, trapz

# Setting up fake data
x = np.sort(np.random.randn(150) * 4 + 4).clip(0,5)
func = lambda x: np.sin(x) * np.cos(x ** 2) + 1
y = func(x)

# Integrating function with upper and lower
# limits of 0 and 5, respectively
fsolution = quad(func, 0, 5)
dsolution = trapz(y, x=x)
```

```
print('fsolution = ' + str(fsolution[0]))
print('dsolution = ' + str(dsolution))
print('The difference is ' + str(np.abs(fsolution[0] - dsolution)))

# fsolution = 5.10034506754
# dsolution = 5.04201628314
# The difference is 0.0583287843989.
```

The quad integrator can only work with a callable function, whereas trapz is a numerical integrator that utilizes data points.

3.4 Statistics

In NumPy there are basic statistical functions like mean, std, median, argmax, and argmin. Moreover, the numpy.arrays have built-in methods that allow us to use most of the NumPy statistics easily.

```
import numpy as np

# Constructing a random array with 1000 elements
x = np.random.randn(1000)

# Calculating several of the built-in methods
# that numpy.array has
mean = x.mean()
std = x.std()
var = x.var()
```

For quick calculations these methods are useful, but more is usually needed for quantitative research. SciPy offers an extended collection of statistical tools such as distributions (continuous or discrete) and functions. We will first cover how to extrapolate the different types of distributions. Afterward, we will discuss the SciPy statistical functions used most often in various fields.

3.4.1 Continuous and Discrete Distributions

There are roughly 80 continuous distributions and over 10 discrete distributions. Twenty of the continuous functions are shown in Figure 3-12 as probability density functions (PDFs) to give a visual impression of what the scipy.stats package provides. These distributions are useful as random number generators, similar to the functions found in numpy.random. Yet the rich variety of functions SciPy provides stands in contrast to the numpy.random functions, which are limited to uniform and Gaussian-like distributions.

When we call a distribution from scipy.stats, we can extract its information in several ways: probability density functions (PDFs), cumulative distribution functions (CDFs), random variable samples (RVSs), percent point functions (PPFs), and more. So how do we set up SciPy to give us these distributions? Working with the classic normal function

$$\mathrm{PDF} = e^{(-x^2/2)/\sqrt{2\pi}} \tag{3.2}$$

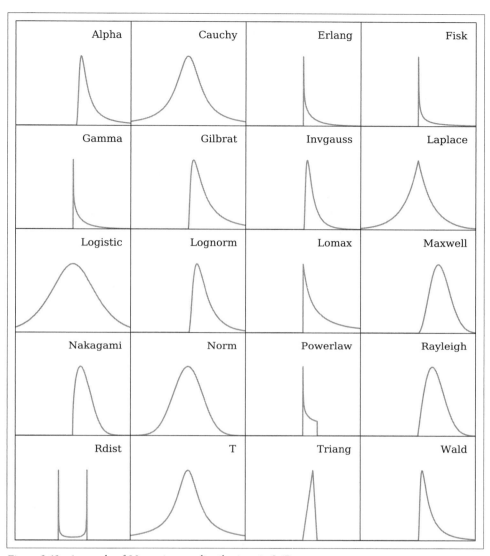

Figure 3-12. A sample of 20 continuous distributions in SciPy.

we demonstrate how to access the distribution.

```
import numpy as np
import scipy.stats import norm

# Set up the sample range
x = np.linspace(-5,5,1000)
```

```
# Here set up the parameters for the normal distribution,
# where loc is the mean and scale is the standard deviation.
dist = norm(loc=0, scale=1)

# Retrieving norm's PDF and CDF
pdf = dist.pdf(x)
cdf = dist.cdf(x)

# Here we draw out 500 random values from the norm.
sample = dist.rvs(500)
```

The distribution can be centered at a different point and scaled with the options `loc` and `scale` as shown in the example. This works as easily with all distributions because of their functional behavior, so it is important to read the documentation[5] when necessary.

In other cases one will need a discrete distribution like the Poisson, binomial, or geometric. Unlike continuous distributions, discrete distributions are useful for problems where a given number of events occur in a fixed interval of time/space, the events occur with a known average rate, and each event is independent of the prior event.

Equation 3.3 is the probability mass function (PMF) of the geometric distribution.

$$PMF = (1 - p)^{(k-1)} \, p \tag{3.3}$$

```
import numpy as np
from scipy.stats import geom

# Here set up the parameters for the geometric distribution.
p = 0.5
dist = geom(p)

# Set up the sample range.
x = np.linspace(0, 5, 1000)

# Retrieving geom's PMF and CDF
pmf = dist.pmf(x)
cdf = dist.cdf(x)

# Here we draw out 500 random values.
sample = dist.rvs(500)
```

3.4.2 Functions

There are more than 60 statistical functions in SciPy, which can be overwhelming to digest if you simply are curious about what is available. The best way to think of the statistics functions is that they either describe or test samples—for example, the frequency of certain values or the Kolmogorov-Smirnov test, respectively.

Since SciPy provides a large range of distributions, it would be great to take advantage of the ones we covered earlier. In the `stats` package, there are a number of functions

---

[5] *http://docs.scipy.org/doc/scipy/reference/stats.html*

such as `kstest` and `normaltest` that test samples. These distribution tests can be very helpful in determining whether a sample comes from some particular distribution or not. Before applying these, be sure you have a good understanding of your data, to avoid misinterpreting the functions' results.

```python
import numpy as np
from scipy import stats

# Generating a normal distribution sample
# with 100 elements
sample = np.random.randn(100)

# normaltest tests the null hypothesis.
out = stats.normaltest(sample)
print('normaltest output')
print('Z-score = ' + str(out[0]))
print('P-value = ' + str(out[1]))

# kstest is the Kolmogorov-Smirnov test for goodness of fit.
# Here its sample is being tested against the normal distribution.
# D is the KS statistic and the closer it is to 0 the better.
out = stats.kstest(sample, 'norm')
print('\nkstest output for the Normal distribution')
print('D = ' + str(out[0]))
print('P-value = ' + str(out[1]))

# Similarly, this can be easily tested against other distributions,
# like the Wald distribution.
out = stats.kstest(sample, 'wald')
print('\nkstest output for the Wald distribution')
print('D = ' + str(out[0]))
print('P-value = ' + str(out[1]))
```

Researchers commonly use descriptive functions for statistics. Some descriptive functions that are available in the `stats` package include the geometric mean (`gmean`), the skewness of a sample (`skew`), and the frequency of values in a sample (`itemfreq`). Using these functions is simple and does not require much input. A few examples follow.

```python
import numpy as np
from scipy import stats

# Generating a normal distribution sample
# with 100 elements
sample = np.random.randn(100)

# The harmonic mean:  Sample values have to
# be greater than 0.
out = stats.hmean(sample[sample > 0])
print('Harmonic mean = ' + str(out))

# The mean, where values below -1 and above 1 are
# removed for the mean calculation
out = stats.tmean(sample, limits=(-1, 1))
print('\nTrimmed mean = ' + str(out))
```

```
# Calculating the skewness of the sample
out = stats.skew(sample)
print('\nSkewness = ' + str(out))

# Additionally, there is a handy summary function called
# describe, which gives a quick look at the data.
out = stats.describe(sample)
print('\nSize = ' + str(out[0]))
print('Min = ' + str(out[1][0]))
print('Max = ' + str(out[1][1]))
print('Mean = ' + str(out[2]))
print('Variance = ' + str(out[3]))
print('Skewness = ' + str(out[4]))
print('Kurtosis = ' + str(out[5]))
```

There are many more functions available in the stats package, so the documentation is worth a look if you need more specific tools. If you need more statistical tools than are available here, try RPy.[6] R is a cornerstone package for statistical analysis, and RPy ports the tools available in that system to Python. If you're content with what is available in SciPy and NumPy but need more automated analysis, then take a look at Pandas.[7] It is a powerful package that can perform quick statistical analysis on big data. Its output is supplied in both numerical values and plots.

3.5   Spatial and Clustering Analysis

From biological to astrophysical sciences, spatial and clustering analysis are key to identifying patterns, groups, and clusters. In biology, for example, the spacing of different plant species hints at how seeds are dispersed, interact with the environment, and grow. In astrophysics, these analysis techniques are used to seek and identify star clusters, galaxy clusters, and large-scale filaments (composed of galaxy clusters). In the computer science domain, identifying and mapping complex networks of nodes and information is a vital study all on its own. With big data and data mining, identifying data clusters is becoming important, in order to organize discovered information, rather than being overwhelmed by it.

 If you need a package that provides good graph theory capabilities, check out NetworkX.[8] It is an excellent Python package for creating, modulating, and studying the structure of complex networks (i.e., minimum spanning trees analysis).

SciPy provides a spatial analysis class (scipy.spatial) and a cluster analysis class (scipy.cluster). The spatial class includes functions to analyze distances between data points (e.g., k-d trees). The cluster class provides two overarching subclasses: vector quantization (vq) and hierarchical clustering (hierarchy). Vector quantization groups

---

[6] *http://rpy.sourceforge.net/*

[7] *http://pandas.pydata.org/*

[8] *http://networkx.lanl.gov/*

large sets of data points (vectors) where each group is represented by centroids. The `hierarchy` subclass contains functions to construct clusters and analyze their substructures.

3.5.1   Vector Quantization

Vector quantization is a general term that can be associated with signal processing, data compression, and clustering. Here we will focus on the clustering component, starting with how to feed data to the **vq** package in order to identify clusters.

```
import numpy as np
from scipy.cluster import vq

# Creating data
c1 = np.random.randn(100, 2) + 5
c2 = np.random.randn(30, 2) - 5
c3 = np.random.randn(50, 2)

# Pooling all the data into one 180 x 2 array
data = np.vstack([c1, c2, c3])

# Calculating the cluster centroids and variance
# from kmeans
centroids, variance = vq.kmeans(data, 3)

# The identified variable contains the information
# we need to separate the points in clusters
# based on the vq function.
identified, distance = vq.vq(data, centroids)

# Retrieving coordinates for points in each vq
# identified core
vqc1 = data[identified == 0]
vqc2 = data[identified == 1]
vqc3 = data[identified == 2]
```

The result of the identified clusters matches up quite well to the original data, as shown in Figure 3-13 (the generated cluster data is on the left and the **vq**-identified clusters are the on the right). But this was done only for data that had little noise. What happens if there is a randomly distributed set of points in the field? The algorithm fails with flying colors. See Figure 3-14 for a nice illustration of this.

3.5.2   Hierarchical Clustering

Hierarchical clustering is a powerful tool for identifying structures that are nested within larger structures. But working with the output can be tricky, as we do not get cleanly identified clusters like we do with the **kmeans** technique. Below is an example[9] wherein we generate a system of multiple clusters. To employ the hierarchy function,

---

[9] The original effort in using this can be found at *http://stackoverflow.com/questions/2982929/plotting-results-of-hierarchical-clustering-ontop-of-a-matrix-of-data-in-python*.

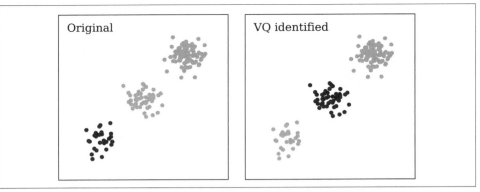

Figure 3-13. Original clusters (left) and `vq.kmeans`*-identified clusters (right). Points are associated to a cluster by color.*

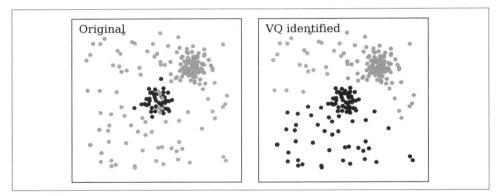

Figure 3-14. Original clusters (left) and `vq.kmeans`*-identified clusters (right). Points are associated to a cluster by color. The uniformly distributed data shows the weak point of the* `vq.kmeans` *function.*

we build a distance matrix, and the output is a dendrogram tree. See Figure 3-15 for a visual example of how hierarchical clustering works.

```
import numpy as np
import matplotlib.pyplot as mpl
from mpl_toolkits.mplot3d import Axes3D
from scipy.spatial.distance import pdist, squareform
import scipy.cluster.hierarchy as hy

# Creating a cluster of clusters function
def clusters(number = 20, cnumber = 5, csize = 10):
    # Note that the way the clusters are positioned is Gaussian randomness.
    rnum = np.random.rand(cnumber, 2)
    rn = rnum[:,0] * number
    rn = rn.astype(int)
    rn[np.where(rn < 5 )] = 5
    rn[np.where(rn > number/2. )] = round(number / 2., 0)
```

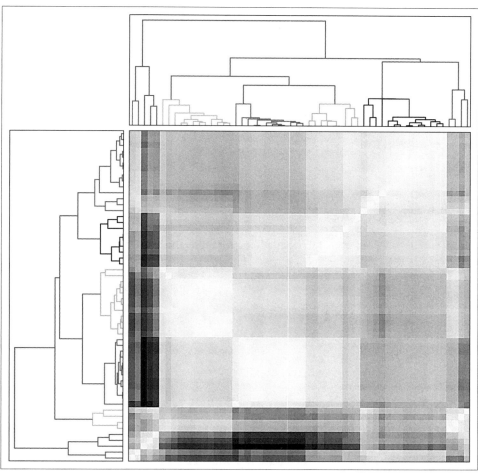

Figure 3-15. The pixelated subplot is the distance matrix, and the two dendrogram subplots show different types of dendrogram methods.

```
ra = rnum[:,1] * 2.9
ra[np.where(ra < 1.5)] = 1.5

cls = np.random.randn(number, 3) * csize

# Random multipliers for central point of cluster
rxyz = np.random.randn(cnumber-1, 3)
for i in xrange(cnumber-1):
    tmp = np.random.randn(rn[i+1], 3)
    x = tmp[:,0] + ( rxyz[i,0] * csize )
    y = tmp[:,1] + ( rxyz[i,1] * csize )
    z = tmp[:,2] + ( rxyz[i,2] * csize )
    tmp = np.column_stack([x,y,z])
    cls = np.vstack([cls,tmp])
return cls
```

```
# Generate a cluster of clusters and distance matrix.
cls = clusters()
D = pdist(cls[:,0:2])
D = squareform(D)

# Compute and plot first dendrogram.
fig = mpl.figure(figsize=(8,8))
ax1 = fig.add_axes([0.09,0.1,0.2,0.6])
Y1 = hy.linkage(D, method='complete')
cutoff = 0.3 * np.max(Y1[:, 2])
Z1 = hy.dendrogram(Y1, orientation='right', color_threshold=cutoff)
ax1.xaxis.set_visible(False)
ax1.yaxis.set_visible(False)

# Compute and plot second dendrogram.
ax2 = fig.add_axes([0.3,0.71,0.6,0.2])
Y2 = hy.linkage(D, method='average')
cutoff = 0.3 * np.max(Y2[:, 2])
Z2 = hy.dendrogram(Y2, color_threshold=cutoff)
ax2.xaxis.set_visible(False)
ax2.yaxis.set_visible(False)

# Plot distance matrix.
ax3 = fig.add_axes([0.3,0.1,0.6,0.6])
idx1 = Z1['leaves']
idx2 = Z2['leaves']
D = D[idx1,:]
D = D[:,idx2]
ax3.matshow(D, aspect='auto', origin='lower', cmap=mpl.cm.YlGnBu)
ax3.xaxis.set_visible(False)
ax3.yaxis.set_visible(False)

# Plot colorbar.
fig.savefig('cluster_hy_f01.pdf', bbox = 'tight')
```

Seeing the distance matrix in the figure with the dendrogram tree highlights how the large and small structures are identified. The question is, how do we distinguish the structures from one another? Here we use a function called fcluster that provides us with the indices to each of the clusters at some threshold. The output from fcluster will depend on the method you use when calculating the linkage function, such as *complete* or *single*. The cutoff value you assign to the cluster is given as the second input in the fcluster function. In the dendrogram function, the cutoff's default is 0.7 * np.max(Y[:, 2]), but here we will use the same cutoff as in the previous example, with the scaler 0.3.

```
# Same imports and cluster function from the previous example
# follow through here.

# Here we define a function to collect the coordinates of
# each point of the different clusters.
def group(data, index):
    number = np.unique(index)
    groups = []
    for i in number:
        groups.append(data[index == i])

    return groups
```

```
# Creating a cluster of clusters
cls = clusters()

# Calculating the linkage matrix
Y = hy.linkage(cls[:,0:2], method='complete')

# Here we use the fcluster function to pull out a
# collection of flat clusters from the hierarchical
# data structure. Note that we are using the same
# cutoff value as in the previous example for the dendrogram
# using the 'complete' method.
cutoff = 0.3 * np.max(Y[:, 2])
index = hy.fcluster(Y, cutoff, 'distance')

# Using the group function, we group points into their
# respective clusters.
groups = group(cls, index)

# Plotting clusters
fig = mpl.figure(figsize=(6, 6))
ax = fig.add_subplot(111)
colors = ['r', 'c', 'b', 'g', 'orange', 'k', 'y', 'gray']
for i, g in enumerate(groups):
    i = np.mod(i, len(colors))
    ax.scatter(g[:,0], g[:,1], c=colors[i], edgecolor='none', s=50)
    ax.xaxis.set_visible(False)
    ax.yaxis.set_visible(False)

fig.savefig('cluster_hy_f02.pdf', bbox = 'tight')
```

The hierarchically identified clusters are shown in Figure 3-16.

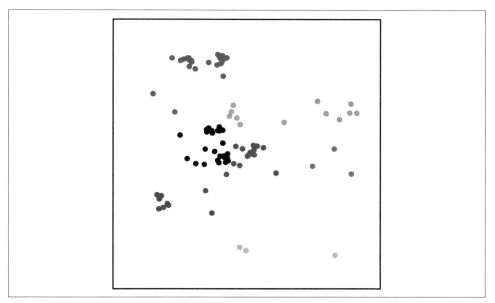

Figure 3-16. Hierarchically identified clusters.

Figure 3-17. A stacked image that is composed of hundreds of exposures from the International Space Station.

3.6   Signal and Image Processing

SciPy allows us to read and write image files like JPEG and PNG images without worrying too much about the file structure for color images. Below, we run through a simple illustration of working with image files to make a nice image[10] (see Figure 3-17) from the International Space Station (ISS).

```
import numpy as np
from scipy.misc import imread, imsave
from glob import glob

# Getting the list of files in the directory
files = glob('space/*.JPG')

# Opening up the first image for loop
im1 = imread(files[0]).astype(np.float32)

# Starting loop and continue co-adding new images
for i in xrange(1, len(files)):
    print i
    im1 += imread(files[i]).astype(np.float32)

# Saving img
imsave('stacked_image.jpg', im1)
```

[10] Original Pythonic effort can be found at *http://stackoverflow.com/questions/9251580/stacking-astronomy-images-with-python*.

Figure 3-18. A stacked image that is composed of hundreds of exposures from the International Space Station.

The JPG images in the Python environment are NumPy arrays with (426, 640, 3), where the three layers are red, green, and blue, respectively.

In the original stacked image, seeing the star trails above Earth is nearly impossible. We modify the previous example to enhance the star trails as shown in Figure 3-18.

```python
import numpy as np
from scipy.misc import imread, imsave
from glob import glob

# This function allows us to place in the
# brightest pixels per x and y position between
# two images. It is similar to PIL's
# ImageChop.Lighter function.
def chop_lighter(image1, image2):
    s1 = np.sum(image1, axis=2)
    s2 = np.sum(image2, axis=2)

    index = s1 < s2
    image1[index, 0] = image2[index, 0]
    image1[index, 1] = image2[index, 1]
    image1[index, 2] = image2[index, 2]
    return image1

# Getting the list of files in the directory
files = glob('space/*.JPG')

# Opening up the first image for looping
im1 = imread(files[0]).astype(np.float32)
im2 = np.copy(im1)
```

```
# Starting loop
for i in xrange(1, len(files)):
    print i
    im = imread(files[i]).astype(np.float32)
    # Same before
    im1 += im
    # im2 shows star trails better
    im2 = chop_lighter(im2, im)

# Saving image with slight tweaking on the combination
# of the two images to show star trails with the
# co-added image.
imsave('stacked_image.jpg', im1/im1.max() + im2/im2.max()*0.2)
```

When dealing with images without SciPy, you have to be more concerned about keeping the array values in the right format when saving them as image files. SciPy deals with that nicely and allows us to focus on processing the images and obtaining our desired effects.

3.7   Sparse Matrices

With NumPy we can operate with reasonable speeds on arrays containing 10^6 elements. Once we go up to 10^7 elements, operations can start to slow down and Python's memory will become limited, depending on the amount of RAM available. What's the best solution if you need to work with an array that is far larger—say, 10^{10} elements? If these massive arrays primarily contain zeros, then you're in luck, as this is the property of *sparse matrices*. If a sparse matrix is treated correctly, operation time and memory usage can go down drastically. The simple example below illustrates this.

 You can determine the byte size of a numpy.array by calling its method nbytes. This can be especially useful when trying to determine what is hogging memory in your code. To do the same with sparse matrices, you can use data.nbytes.

```
import numpy as np
from scipy.sparse.linalg import eigsh
from scipy.linalg import eigh
import scipy.sparse
import time

N = 3000
# Creating a random sparse matrix
m = scipy.sparse.rand(N, N)

# Creating an array clone of it
a = m.toarray()

print('The numpy array data size: ' + str(a.nbytes) + ' bytes')
print('The sparse matrix data size: ' + str(m.data.nbytes) + ' bytes')

# Non-sparse
t0 = time.time()
```

```
res1 = eigh(a)
dt = str(np.round(time.time() - t0, 3)) + ' seconds'
print('Non-sparse operation takes ' + dt)

# Sparse
t0 = time.time()
res2 = eigsh(m)
dt = str(np.round(time.time() - t0, 3)) + ' seconds'
print('Sparse operation takes ' + dt)
```

The memory allotted to the NumPy array and sparse matrix were 68 MB and 0.68 MB, respectively. In the same order, the times taken to process the Eigen commands were 36.6 and 0.2 seconds on my computer. This means that the sparse matrix was 100 times more memory efficient and the Eigen operation was roughly 150 times faster than the non-sparse cases.

 If you're unfamiliar with sparse matrices, I suggest reading *http://www .scipy.org/SciPyPackages/Sparse*, where the basics on sparse matrices and operations are discussed.

In 2D and 3D geometry, there are many sparse data structures used in fields like engineering, computational fluid dynamics, electromagnetism, thermodynamics, and acoustics. Non-geometric instances of sparse matrices are applicable to optimization, economic modeling, mathematics and statistics, and network/graph theories.

Using `scipy.io`, you can read and write common sparse matrix file formats such as Matrix Market and Harwell-Boeing, or load MatLab files. This is especially useful for collaborations with others who use these data formats. In the next section, we expand on these `scipy.io` capabilities.

3.8   Reading and Writing Files Beyond NumPy

NumPy provides a good set of input and output capabilities with ASCII files. Its binary support is great if you only need to share information to be read from one Python environment to another. But what about more universally used binary file formats? If you are using Matlab or collaborating with others who are using it, then as briefly mentioned in the previous section, it is not a problem for NumPy to read and write Matlab-supported files (using `scipy.io.loadmat` and `scipy.savemat`).

In fields like astronomy, geography, and medicine, there is a programming language called IDL. It saves files in a binary format and can be read by NumPy using a built-in package called `scipy.io.readsav`. It is a flexible and fast module, but it does not have writing capabilities.

Last but not least, you can query, read, and write Matrix Market files. These are very commonly used to share matrix data structures that are written in ASCII format. This format is well supported in other languages like C, Fortran, and Matlab, so it is a good format to use due to its universality and user readability. It is also suitable for sparse matrices.

## CHAPTER 4

SciKit: Taking SciPy One Step Further

SciPy and NumPy are great tools and provide us with most of the functionality that we need. Sometimes, though we need more advanced tools, and that's where the scikits come in. These are a set of packages that are complementary to SciPy. There are currently more than 20 scikit packages available; a list can be found at *http://scikit .appspot.com/*. Here we will go over two well-maintained and popular packages: Scikit-image, a more beefed-up image module than `scipy.ndimage`, is aimed to be an imaging processing toolkit for SciPy. Scikit-learn is a machine learning package that can be used for a range of scientific and engineering purposes.

4.1 Scikit-Image

SciPy's `ndimage` class contains many useful tools for processing multi-dimensional data, such as basic filtering (e.g., Gaussian smoothing), Fourier transform, morphology (e.g., binary erosion), interpolation, and measurements. From those functions we can write programs to execute more complex operations. Scikit-image has fortunately taken on the task of going a step further to provide more advanced functions that we may need for scientific research. These advanced and high-level modules include color space conversion, image intensity adjustment algorithms, feature detections, filters for sharpening and denoising, read/write capabilities, and more.

4.1.1 Dynamic Threshold

A common application in imaging science is segmenting image components from one another, which is referred to as thresholding. The classic thresholding technique works well when the background of the image is flat. Unfortunately, this situation is not the norm; instead, the background visually will be changing throughout the image. Hence, adaptive thresholding techniques have been developed, and we can easily utilize them in scikit-image. In the following example, we generate an image with a non-uniform background that has randomly placed fuzzy dots throughout (see Figure 4-1). Then

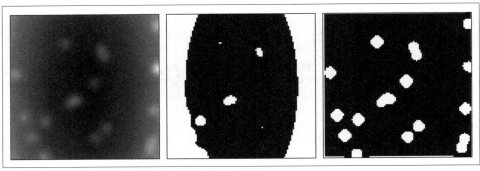

Figure 4-1. Illustration of thresholding. The original synthetic image is on the left, with classic and dynamic threshold algorithms at work from middle to right, respectively.

we run a basic and adaptive threshold function on the image to see how well we can segment the fuzzy dots from the background.

```python
import numpy as np
import matplotlib.pyplot as mpl
import scipy.ndimage as ndimage
import skimage.filter as skif

# Generating data points with a non-uniform background
x = np.random.uniform(low=0, high=100, size=20).astype(int)
y = np.random.uniform(low=0, high=100, size=20).astype(int)

# Creating image with non-uniform background
func = lambda x, y: x**2 + y**2
grid_x, grid_y = np.mgrid[-1:1:100j, -2:2:100j]
bkg = func(grid_x, grid_y)
bkg = bkg / np.max(bkg)

# Creating points
clean = np.zeros((100,100))
clean[(x,y)] += 5
clean = ndimage.gaussian_filter(clean, 3)
clean = clean / np.max(clean)

# Combining both the non-uniform background
# and points
fimg = bkg + clean
fimg = fimg / np.max(fimg)

# Defining minimum neighboring size of objects
block_size = 3

# Adaptive threshold function which returns image
# map of structures that are different relative to
# background
adaptive_cut = skif.threshold_adaptive(fimg, block_size, offset=0)
```

```
# Global threshold
global_thresh = skif.threshold_otsu(fimg)
global_cut = fimg > global_thresh

# Creating figure to highlight difference between
# adaptive and global threshold methods
fig = mpl.figure(figsize=(8, 4))
fig.subplots_adjust(hspace=0.05, wspace=0.05)

ax1 = fig.add_subplot(131)
ax1.imshow(fimg)
ax1.xaxis.set_visible(False)
ax1.yaxis.set_visible(False)

ax2 = fig.add_subplot(132)
ax2.imshow(global_cut)
ax2.xaxis.set_visible(False)
ax2.yaxis.set_visible(False)

ax3 = fig.add_subplot(133)
ax3.imshow(adaptive_cut)
ax3.xaxis.set_visible(False)
ax3.yaxis.set_visible(False)

fig.savefig('scikit_image_f01.pdf', bbox_inches='tight')
```

In this case, as shown in Figure 4-1, the adaptive thresholding technique (right panel) obviously works far better than the basic one (middle panel). Most of the code above is for generating the image and plotting the output for context. The actual code for adaptively thresholding the image took only two lines.

4.1.2 Local Maxima

Approaching a slightly different problem, but with a similar setup as before, how can we identify points on a non-uniform background to obtain their pixel coordinates? Here we can use `skimage.morphology.is_local_maximum`, which only needs the image as a default input. The function works surprisingly well; see Figure 4-2, where the identified maxima are circled in blue.

```
import numpy as np
import matplotlib.pyplot as mpl
import scipy.ndimage as ndimage
import skimage.morphology as morph

# Generating data points with a non-uniform background
x = np.random.uniform(low=0, high=200, size=20).astype(int)
y = np.random.uniform(low=0, high=400, size=20).astype(int)

# Creating image with non-uniform background
func = lambda x, y: np.cos(x)+ np.sin(y)
grid_x, grid_y = np.mgrid[0:12:200j, 0:24:400j]
bkg = func(grid_x, grid_y)
bkg = bkg / np.max(bkg)
```

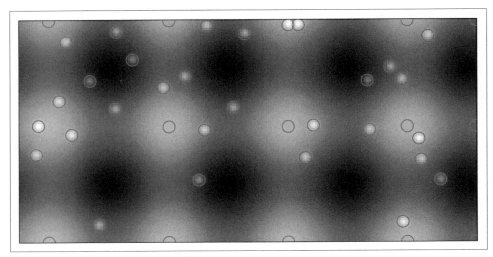

Figure 4-2. Identified local maxima (blue circles).

```
# Creating points
clean = np.zeros((200,400))
clean[(x,y)] += 5
clean = ndimage.gaussian_filter(clean, 3)
clean = clean / np.max(clean)

# Combining both the non-uniform background
# and points
fimg = bkg + clean
fimg = fimg / np.max(fimg)

# Calculating local maxima
lm1 = morph.is_local_maximum(fimg)
x1, y1 = np.where(lm1.T == True)

# Creating figure to show local maximum detection
# rate success
fig = mpl.figure(figsize=(8, 4))

ax = fig.add_subplot(111)
ax.imshow(fimg)
ax.scatter(x1, y1, s=100, facecolor='none', edgecolor='#009999')
ax.set_xlim(0,400)
ax.set_ylim(0,200)
ax.xaxis.set_visible(False)
ax.yaxis.set_visible(False)

fig.savefig('scikit_image_f02.pdf', bbox_inches='tight')
```

If you look closely at the figure, you will notice that there are identified maxima that do not point to fuzzy sources but instead to the background peaks. These peaks are a problem, but by definition this is what skimage.morphology.is_local_maximum will find. How can we filter out these "false positives"? Since we have the coordinates of the local maxima, we can look for properties that will differentiate the sources from the rest. The background is relatively smooth compared to the sources, so we could differentiate them easily by standard deviation from the peaks to their local neighboring pixels.

How does scikit-image fare with real-world research problems? Quite well, in fact. In astronomy, the flux per unit area received from stars can be measured in images by quantifying intensity levels at their locations—a process called photometry. Photometry has been done for quite some time in multiple programming languages, but there is no de facto package for Python yet. The first step in photometry is identifying the stars. In the following example, we will use is_local_maximum to identify sources (hopefully stars) in a stellar cluster called NGC 3603 that was observed with the Hubble Space Telescope. Note that one additional package, PyFITS,[1] is used here. It is a standard astronomical package for loading binary data stored in FITS[2] format.

```python
import numpy as np
import pyfits
import matplotlib.pyplot as mpl
import skimage.morphology as morph
import skimage.exposure as skie

# Loading astronomy image from an infrared space telescope
img = pyfits.getdata('stellar_cluster.fits')[500:1500, 500:1500]

# Prep file scikit-image environment and plotting
limg = np.arcsinh(img)
limg = limg / limg.max()
low = np.percentile(limg, 0.25)
high = np.percentile(limg, 99.5)
opt_img = skie.exposure.rescale_intensity(limg, in_range=(low, high))

# Calculating local maxima and filtering out noise
lm = morph.is_local_maximum(limg)
x1, y1 = np.where(lm.T == True)
v = limg[(y1, x1)]
lim = 0.5
x2, y2 = x1[v > lim], y1[v > lim]

# Creating figure to show local maximum detection
# rate success
fig = mpl.figure(figsize=(8,4))
fig.subplots_adjust(hspace=0.05, wspace=0.05)

ax1 = fig.add_subplot(121)
ax1.imshow(opt_img)
ax1.set_xlim(0, img.shape[1])
ax1.set_ylim(0, img.shape[0])
ax1.xaxis.set_visible(False)
ax1.yaxis.set_visible(False)
```

[1] http://www.stsci.edu/institute/software_hardware/pyfits

[2] http://heasarc.nasa.gov/docs/heasarc/fits.html

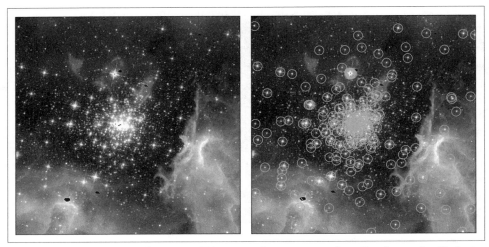

Figure 4-3. Stars (orange circles) in a Hubble Space Telescope image of a stellar cluster, identified using the is_local_maximum *function.*

```
ax2 = fig.add_subplot(122)
ax2.imshow(opt_img)
ax2.scatter(x2, y2, s=80, facecolor='none', edgecolor='#FF7400')
ax2.set_xlim(0, img.shape[1])
ax2.set_ylim(0, img.shape[0])
ax2.xaxis.set_visible(False)
ax2.yaxis.set_visible(False)

fig.savefig('scikit_image_f03.pdf', bbox_inches='tight')
```

The skimage.morphology.is_local_maximum function returns over 30,000 local maxima in the image, and many of the detections are false positives. We apply a simple threshold value to get rid of any maxima peaks that have a pixel value below 0.5 (from the normalized image) to bring that number down to roughly 200. There are much better ways to filter out non-stellar maxima (e.g., noise), but we will still stick with the current method for simplicity. In Figure 4-3 we can see that the detections are good overall. Once we know where the stars are, we can apply flux measurement algorithms, but that goes beyond the scope of this chapter.

Hopefully, with this brief overview of what is available in the scikit-image package, you already have a good idea of how it can be used for your objectives.

4.2 Scikit-Learn

Possibly the most extensive scikit is scikit-learn. It is an easy-to-use machine learning bundle that contains a collection of tools associated with supervised and unsupervised learning. Some of you may be asking, "So what can machine learning help me do that I could not do before?" One word: predictions.

Let us assume that we are given a problem where there is a good sample of empirical data at hand: can predictions be made about it? To figure this out, we would try to create an analytical model to describe the data, though that does not always work due to complex dependencies. But what if you could feed that data to a machine, teach the machine what is good and bad about the data, and then let it provide its own predictions? That is what machine learning is. If used right, it can be very powerful.

Not only is the scikit-learn package impressive, but its documentation is generous and well organized[3]. Rather than reinventing the wheel to show what scikit-learn is, I'm going to take several examples that we did in prior sections and see if scikit-learn could provide better and more elegant solutions. This method of implementing scikit-learn is aimed to inspire you as to how the package could be applied to your own research.

4.2.1 Linear Regression

In Chapter 3 we fitted a line to a dataset, which is a linear regression problem. If we are dealing with data that has a higher number of dimensions, how do we go about a linear regression solution? Scikit-learn has a large number of tools to do this, such as Lasso and ridge regression. For now we will stick with the ordinary least squares regression function, which solves mathematical problems of the form

$$\min_{w} \| X \beta - y \| \tag{4.1}$$

where w is the set of coefficients. The number of coefficients depends on the number of dimensions in the data, $N(\text{coeff}) = M\text{D} - 1$, where $M > 1$ and is an integer. In the example below we are computing the linear regression of a plane in 3D space, so there are two coefficients to solve for. Here we show how to use LinearRegression to train the model with data, approximate a best fit, give a prediction from the data, and test other data (test) to see how well it fits the model. A visual output of the linear regression is shown in Figure 4-4.

```
import numpy as np
import matplotlib.pyplot as mpl
from mpl_toolkits.mplot3d import Axes3D
from sklearn import linear_model
from sklearn.datasets.samples_generator import make_regression

# Generating synthetic data for training and testing
X, y = make_regression(n_samples=100, n_features=2, n_informative=1,\
                       random_state=0, noise=50)

# X and y are values for 3D space. We first need to train
# the machine, so we split X and y into X_train, X_test,
# y_train, and y_test. The *_train data will be given to the
# model to train it.
X_train, X_test = X[:80], X[-20:]
y_train, y_test = y[:80], y[-20:]
```

[3] http://scikit-learn.org/

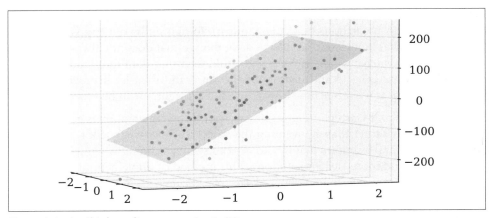

Figure 4-4. A scikit-learn linear regression in 3D space.

```
# Creating instance of model
regr = linear_model.LinearRegression()

# Training the model
regr.fit(X_train, y_train)

# Printing the coefficients
print(regr.coef_)
# [-10.25691752  90.5463984 ]

# Predicting y-value based on training
X1 = np.array([1.2, 4])
print(regr.predict(X1))
# 350.860363861

# With the *_test data we can see how the result matches
# the data the model was trained with.
# It should be a good match as the *_train and *_test
# data come from the same sample. Output: 1 is perfect
# prediction and anything lower is worse.
print(regr.score(X_test, y_test))
# 0.949827492261

fig = mpl.figure(figsize=(8, 5))
ax = fig.add_subplot(111, projection='3d')
# ax = Axes3D(fig)

# Data
ax.scatter(X_train[:,0], X_train[:,1], y_train, facecolor='#00CC00')
ax.scatter(X_test[:,0], X_test[:,1], y_test, facecolor='#FF7800')

# Function with coefficient variables
coef = regr.coef_
line = lambda x1, x2: coef[0] * x1 + coef[1] * x2
```

```
grid_x1, grid_x2 = np.mgrid[-2:2:10j, -2:2:10j]
ax.plot_surface(grid_x1, grid_x2, line(grid_x1, grid_x2),
                alpha=0.1, color='k')
ax.xaxis.set_visible(False)
ax.yaxis.set_visible(False)
ax.zaxis.set_visible(False)
fig.savefig('scikit_learn_regression.pdf', bbox='tight')
```

This `LinearRegression` function can work with much higher dimensions, so dealing with a larger number of inputs in a model is straightforward. It is advisable to look at the other linear regression models[4] as well, as they may be more appropriate for your data.

4.2.2 Clustering

SciPy has two packages for cluster analysis with vector quantization (`kmeans`) and hierarchy. The `kmeans` method was the easier of the two for implementing and segmenting data into several components based on their spatial characteristics. Scikit-learn provides a set of tools[5] to do more cluster analysis that goes beyond what SciPy has. For a suitable comparison to the `kmeans` function in SciPy, the `DBSCAN` algorithm is used in the following example. `DBSCAN` works by finding core points that have many data points within a given radius. Once the core is defined, the process is iteratively computed until there are no more core points definable within the maximum radius? This algorithm does exceptionally well compared to `kmeans` where there is noise present in the data.

```
import numpy as np
import matplotlib.pyplot as mpl
from scipy.spatial import distance
from sklearn.cluster import DBSCAN

# Creating data
c1 = np.random.randn(100, 2) + 5
c2 = np.random.randn(50, 2)

# Creating a uniformly distributed background
u1 = np.random.uniform(low=-10, high=10, size=100)
u2 = np.random.uniform(low=-10, high=10, size=100)
c3 = np.column_stack([u1, u2])

# Pooling all the data into one 150 x 2 array
data = np.vstack([c1, c2, c3])

# Calculating the cluster with DBSCAN function.
# db.labels_ is an array with identifiers to the
# different clusters in the data.
db = DBSCAN().fit(data, eps=0.95, min_samples=10)
labels = db.labels_
```

---

[4] *http://www.scikit-learn.org/stable/modules/linear_model.html*

[5] *http://www.scikit-learn.org/stable/modules/clustering.html*

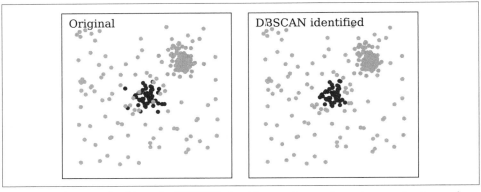

Figure 4-5. An example of how the DBSCAN algorithm excels over the vector quantization package in SciPy. The uniformly distributed points are not included as cluster members.

```
# Retrieving coordinates for points in each
# identified core. There are two clusters
# denoted as 0 and 1 and the noise is denoted
# as -1. Here we split the data based on which
# component they belong to.
dbc1 = data[labels == 0]
dbc2 = data[labels == 1]
noise = data[labels == -1]

# Setting up plot details
x1, x2 = -12, 12
y1, y2 = -12, 12

fig = mpl.figure()
fig.subplots_adjust(hspace=0.1, wspace=0.1)

ax1 = fig.add_subplot(121, aspect='equal')
ax1.scatter(c1[:,0], c1[:,1], lw=0.5, color='#00CC00')
ax1.scatter(c2[:,0], c2[:,1], lw=0.5, color='#028E9B')
ax1.scatter(c3[:,0], c3[:,1], lw=0.5, color='#FF7800')
ax1.xaxis.set_visible(False)
ax1.yaxis.set_visible(False)
ax1.set_xlim(x1, x2)
ax1.set_ylim(y1, y2)
ax1.text(-11, 10, 'Original')

ax2 = fig.add_subplot(122, aspect='equal')
ax2.scatter(dbc1[:,0], dbc1[:,1], lw=0.5, color='#00CC00')
ax2.scatter(dbc2[:,0], dbc2[:,1], lw=0.5, color='#028E9B')
ax2.scatter(noise[:,0], noise[:,1], lw=0.5, color='#FF7800')
ax2.xaxis.set_visible(False)
ax2.yaxis.set_visible(False)
ax2.set_xlim(x1, x2)
ax2.set_ylim(y1, y2)
ax2.text(-11, 10, 'DBSCAN identified')

fig.savefig('scikit_learn_clusters.pdf', bbox_inches='tight')
```

Nearly all the data points originally defined to be part of the clusters are retained, and the noisy background data points are excluded (see Figure 4-5). This highlights the advantage of DBSCAN over kmeans when data that should not be part of a cluster is present in a sample. This obviously is dependent on the spatial characteristics of the given distributions.

## CHAPTER 5

Conclusion

5.1 Summary

This book is meant to help you as the reader to become familiar with SciPy and NumPy and to walk away with tools that you can use for your own research. The online documentation for SciPy and NumPy is comprehensive, and it takes time to sort out what you want from the packages. We all want to learn new tools and use them with as little time and effort possible. Hopefully, this book was able to do that for you.

We have covered how to utilize NumPy arrays for array indexing, math operations, and loading and saving data. With SciPy, we went over tools that are important for scientific research, such as optimization, interpolation, integration, clustering, statistics, and more. The bulk of the material we discussed was on SciPy since there are so many modules in it.

As a bonus, we learned about two powerful scikit packages. Scikit-image is a powerful package that extends beyond the imaging capabilities of SciPy. With scikit-learn, we demonstrated how to employ machine learning to solve problems that would have been otherwise tough to solve.

5.2 What's Next?

You are now familiar with SciPy, NumPy, and two scikit packages. The functions and tools we covered should allow you to comfortably approach your research investigations with more confidence. Moreover, using these resources, you probably see new ways of solving problems that you were not aware of before. If you're looking for more (e.g., indefinite integrals), then you should look for other packages. A good online resource is the PyPI website,[1] where thousands of packages are registered. You can simply browse through to find what you're looking for.

---

[1] *http://pypi.python.org/pypi*

Also, joining Python mailing lists associated with your field of research is a good idea. You will see many discussions among other Python users and may find what you need. Or just ask a question yourself on these lists. Another good information repository is *stackoverflow.com*, which is a central hub where programmers can ask questions, find answers, and provide solutions to programming-related problems.

About the Author

Eli Bressert was born in Tucson, Arizona. He worked as a science imager for NASA's Chandra X-ray Space Telescope, optimizing science images that are frequently seen on book covers, newspapers, television, and other media. Afterward, Eli obtained his PhD in astrophysics at the University of Exeter and is currently a Bolton Fellow at CSIRO Astronomy and Space Science in Sydney, Australia. For the last six years, Eli has been programming in Python and giving Python lectures at Harvard University, the European Space Astronomy Centre, and the European Southern Observatory. He is one of the founding developers of two well-known astrophysics Python packages: ATpy and APLpy.

Get even more for your money.

Join the O'Reilly Community, and register the O'Reilly books you own. It's free, and you'll get:

- $4.99 ebook upgrade offer
- 40% upgrade offer on O'Reilly print books
- Membership discounts on books and events
- Free lifetime updates to ebooks and videos
- Multiple ebook formats, DRM FREE
- Participation in the O'Reilly community
- Newsletters
- Account management
- 100% Satisfaction Guarantee

Signing up is easy:

1. **Go to: oreilly.com/go/register**
2. **Create an O'Reilly login.**
3. **Provide your address.**
4. **Register your books.**

Note: English-language books only

To order books online:
oreilly.com/store

For questions about products or an order:
orders@oreilly.com

To sign up to get topic-specific email announcements and/or news about upcoming books, conferences, special offers, and new technologies:
elists@oreilly.com

For technical questions about book content:
booktech@oreilly.com

To submit new book proposals to our editors:
proposals@oreilly.com

O'Reilly books are available in multiple DRM-free ebook formats. For more information:
oreilly.com/ebooks

O'REILLY®

Spreading the knowledge of innovators   oreilly.com